CONTENTS

PREFACE

Spiritual minds are convinced that we live in days of advanced Satanism. As the god of this world, Satan is succeeding in flooding his domain with an ever-growing number of pleasures and pursuits. Souls must not be given time to think. And how occupied the worldling is!

And then these are days when people have cast off all restraint. Gone are the days when reserve held sway. Things that would have shocked our grandparents are now commonplace and taken for granted. We live in an age of unwholesome suggestiveness. The world is given over to sin! *Rotten* is a mild word to describe the moral condition of civilization. And we hold Satan responsible for the corruption in the world.

It is, therefore, imperative for the saints of God to understand the devices of the enemy in these last days. A thorough understanding of Satan and his works forces one to look out upon these tangled times with different eyes.

In the compass of this somewhat unusual book, as some would think, I have sought to trace the diabolical plan of Satan through the ages. Others have labored in this field of study, and, entering into their labors, I have herewith set forth the fruits of a meditation that has strengthened my faith in the coming overthrow of the usurper.

—*Herbert Lockyer*

SATAN THE ANTICHRIST, OR THE ROYAL SEED

From first to last, the Bible is a book of battles. God strives against man. Man defies God. Satan engages in deadly conflict with both God and man; and both man and God are found arrayed against their mutual archenemy, the devil. Man is also seen at war with man.

But the devil stands before us upon the pages of Holy Writ as the bitterest foe of heaven and earth. No matter where you turn, you find this created, personal, evil once represented as the adversary of God and man, of Christ and the Christian.

In fact, it is very interesting to think of God's Word as a record of the devil's antagonism to forces, human and heavenly, and studying such with spirit-anointed eyes, discover, thereby, the wiles and stratagems of Satan to overthrow the eternal counsels and purposes of God; and then to behold how gloriously he is defeated at every point by One who is "greater than he."

The purpose of this present study is to show how Satan is portrayed in Scripture as the great antagonist of our Lord Jesus Christ. That he bore intense hatred to God's beloved Son from the beginning of his evil career is evident to all who read their Bible with any purpose, seeing that such a theme forms a great and important subject of biblical study.

Into the truths of Satan's preexistence and personality, we are not venturing, as such are taken for granted at this stage.

It will be observed that we are naming our study *Satan and the Antichrist*. True it is that all who deny the Father and the Son are antichrists (see 1 John 2:22), as well as those who deny the incarnation of our Lord (see 1 John 4:3; 2 John 1:7).

It is also true that there are many antichrists abroad today; and that "*the man of sin*" (2 Thessalonians 2:3) of the tribulation period will be known as "*that antichrist*" (1 John 2:18), so called because he will be energized by the devil himself to lead the world in rebellion and antagonism to our Lord.

But seeing that Satan is at the back of all anti-Christian forces, and the instigator of all open hatred to God and to His Christ, he can be fitly termed—Satan, the antichrist.

Before pursuing our study, it may be as well to utter one word regarding the levity even among Christian people when speaking of the devil and his works. No one with any conception of the danger that he is to us, and to the cause we represent, can ever speak of him in a jocular way, or engage in flippant conversation regarding his personality and work. All unwarranted appellations such as "Old Nick" or "Black Face" are to be deprecated.

It behooves us to follow the example of Michael in his manner of dealing with Satan. When the archangel came into conflict with him, he spoke respectfully to him, remembering his previous glory and dignity. (See Zechariah 3:1–2; Jude 9.)

PART I

BEFORE THE CHURCH PERIOD

It may be somewhat instructive if we try to give a brief survey of our theme, before examining it more particularly. Satan's rebellion in the realm of angelic beings, over which he had control, caused God to destroy their habitable world so that it became *"without form, and void"* (Genesis 1:2). God then restored the earth He had devastated because of Satan's revolt, making it fair and beautiful so that He might fill it with sinless beings who would do His will.

But with this plan of God there followed another attempt on Satan's part to frustrate the desire of the Almighty, for the devil became, from the moment of the earth's re-creation and man's creation, the direct antagonist of both God and man. He immediately set out with all the wisdom he possessed to make man into a sinner like himself. He determined that since *"everlasting fire…for the devil and his angels"* (Matthew 25:41), then this selfsame devil will devise every means to drag mankind down with him. And, alas, from the beginning of our world, he has often succeeded.

With man's defeat by the devil, there came the immediate promise of *redemption*. From the woman beguiled by the deceiver, one was to spring who would overthrow the devil's kingdom, destroy his works, and make man *"more than conquerors"* (Romans 8:37). And our present study will show how Satan, from the time of the first pronouncement in Genesis 3:15, set out to thwart God's redemption plan; and how, having failed to meddle in our Redeemer's ancestry throughout the Old Testament, as well as in our Lord's physical and resurrection body in the New Testament, he continues his antagonism against our Lord's mystical body, the church, throughout the succeeding ages.

Dealing, then, in the first place with the unfolding of Satan's diabolical purpose to checkmate God's redeeming purpose before the church period, our minds naturally turn to that portion of Scripture in which the truth of the church, as the body of Christ, is not fully unfolded—namely, the Old Testament and the four gospels.

THE OLD TESTAMENT

Although it is true that the Old Testament does not give us an adequate conception of the devil's personality and works, yet sufficient is revealed to indicate his determination to block God's promise regarding the sending of His Son into the world as its Savior. And, as we shall see, Satan employed many devices and arts to destroy the "Seed" that would ultimately produce Christ, his great antagonist and glorious Conqueror.

THE HUMAN RACE

Let us endeavor to trace the subtle workings of Satan from the time of Adam to Noah, which is the "primeval period" of biblical and human history.

THE FIRST HUMAN PAIR

Satan's antagonism toward God commenced the moment God sought to populate the earth with beings fashioned in His own image. Of course, Satan's own personal revolt and hatred commenced when God deposed him, but here in Genesis 3, we have the first recorded attempt of Satan to overthrow the purpose of God regarding man. And as one writer has pointed out, in each case, the human instrument had his own personal interest to serve, while Satan had his own great object in view. Hence, God had, in each case, to interfere and avert the evil and the danger of which His servants and people were wholly ignorant.

SATAN'S ANTAGONISM TOWARD GOD COMMENCED THE MOMENT GOD SOUGHT TO POPULATE THE EARTH WITH BEINGS FASHIONED IN HIS OWN IMAGE.

HE BEGINS WITH EVE

The first title given to our adversary is highly suggestive, namely, "*the serpent*" (Genesis 3:1). Here, at the very beginning of our Bible, God tears the mask from Satan, revealing him in all his cunning subtlety and cruel deception. He came to Eve with the smooth, covered suggestion of doubt. She had received the divine prohibition regarding "*the tree of the knowledge of good and evil*" (Genesis 2:17), but Satan succeeds in bringing Adam's wife under his sway, thus making her the first human sinner in God's restored universe.

HE THEN REACHES ADAM

Because influence is never neutral, Adam quickly succumbs to the subtle purpose of Satan, who, through Eve, reaches her helpmate. This causes the first human pair to fall, thus producing the terrible sorrow and disaster that have marred human lives ever since. And so, the opening chapter of human history tells us that Satan succeeded in marring not only the angelic harmony, as witnessed in the fall of the angels, but also the discord that has existed ever since Eden between God and man.

THE CURSE AND REDEMPTION

With the fall of man comes the promise of redemption. It is only as we realize the inner significance of Genesis 3:14–15, where begins "the highway of the seed," that we can begin to follow the age-long antagonism between Christ and Satan. In the bruising of the heel, that is, the lower-most part, you have the temporary sufferings of the Seed; but in the bruising of the "head," that is, the most vital part, you have the complete destruction of Satan and his works by Christ, the Victor Divine. Let us tarry over two things at this point:

THE SERPENT

In Genesis 3:14, God curses the serpent, that is, the vehicle used by the devil for the accomplishment of his crafty plan. And, strange to say, Satan is the first to receive the promise of redemption. What irony! Now the serpent in his edenic form is not to be thought of as a writhing reptile. That is the effect of the curse. The creature that lent itself to Satan may well have been the most beautiful, as it was the most subtle of creatures less than man. Traces of that beauty remain, despite the curse. Every movement of a serpent is graceful and many species are beautifully colored. In the serpent, Satan first appeared as *"an angel of light"* (2 Corinthians 11:14). And this language is easily understood when we remember that possibly God originally made the serpent with legs. The serpent is the only animal with a long skeleton that moves upon its body. We also realize the force of the phrase *"it shall bruise thy head"* (Genesis 3:15) when we remember the fact that the serpent's chief care of itself is for its head, because the heart of a serpent is under its throat.

And to the foregoing word of Dr. Schofield, we can add that in the curse pronounced against the serpent, sentence was also passed upon the devil himself. The language used foreshadows his utmost humiliation.

THE SEED

In the first great promise and prophecy of redemption in Genesis 3:15, we have the first link in the long chain of Satan's antagonism. With this gracious word, a window was opened into heaven, and the devil saw, as he had never seen before, something of the matchless grace and boundless love of God.

Knowing something of what the deliverance of man from sin would involve, and that God would preserve the messianic line through the ages until, in the fullness of time, the Deliverer should be born of a woman, Satan commenced his enmity against God and man. As soon as his doom was pronounced, he set out to strive, in every age and in every way, to thwart God's messianic plan of ultimately producing the One from the woman's seed who would utterly and finally destroy the works of the devil.

THE FIRST HUMAN FAMILY

It is most interesting to observe how God defeats the crafty purpose of Satan at every point. For example, how disappointed he must have been when he discovered that although God severely punished

GOD DID NOT CONSIGN ADAM AND EVE TO THE ULTIMATE DOOM THEIR SIN DESERVED. WITH JUDGMENT, THERE WAS GRACE, FOR IN THE PROMISED SEED, ALL THE SONS AND DAUGHTERS OF ADAM'S GRACE CAN FIND THEIR WAY BACK TO GOD.

our first parents, He did not consign them to the ultimate doom their sin deserved. With judgment, there was grace, for in the promised Seed, all the sons and daughters of Adam's grace can find their way back to God.

Well as Satan's efforts with our first parents failed from the divine standpoint, he speedily concentrates his hatred on their immediate seed and offspring. And so we reach his next stage of antagonism.

"Cain rose up against Abel his brother, and slew him" (Genesis 4:8). Abel is a type of the spiritual man. His name, meaning "that which ascends," describes the tenor of his life. The character of his offering, *"the firstlings of his flock"* (Genesis 4:4), a foreshadowing of God's "firstling," Jesus, Satan's master and conqueror, made Abel not only acceptable to God but also a fitting successor to Adam in the ancestry of our Redeemer.

But Cain slew Abel, and at the back of Cain's anger, there was the diabolical antagonism of the devil. Here we have his first attempt to destroy "the royal Seed." And was it not this very treacherous act that led our Lord to call him *"a murderer from the beginning"* (John 8:44)?

But again we find that God not only rules, but overrules, and so, to continue the "seed" of Genesis 3:15, Eve bears Seth. *"For God, said she, hath appointed me another seed instead of Abel"* (Genesis 4:25). And Seth, we are reminded, means "substitution." Surely this must have been another reminder to the devil that the substitutionary work of the cross was the weapon God meant to use for his overthrow.

THE FIRST HUMAN GENERATION

Anyone reading the sixth chapter of Genesis can readily see how the desperation of Satan becomes more intense, and how his hatred grows as he discovers that God's omnipotent power is being matched against him. Through those first centuries of our world's history, Satan's poison spreads through the veins of society until we read that *"the wickedness of man was great in the earth, and that every imagination of the thoughts of his heart was only evil continually"* (Genesis 6:5). Such an estimation of sin was not from any human standpoint but from the divine, for it was God who witnessed it.

What desolation and degradation! How complete was the ruin of the first generation! "*The earth also was corrupt before God, and the earth was filled with violence*" (verse 11). If it be true that "*the sons of God*" of Genesis 6:2 were among "*the angels which kept not their first estate*" (Jude 1:6), and that their union with "*the daughters of men*" (Genesis 6:2) led to the production of the "*mighty men*" who evidently were "*giants*" (verse 4), masters in iniquity and superhuman in size and character, then one can begin to appreciate God's solemn vow in verse 7: "*I will destroy man whom I have created from the face of the earth.*"

What pleasure must have broken over Satan's evil heart when he heard such a decree! "*The end of all flesh is come before me*" (Genesis 6:13). Has the arch-foe of mankind succeeded? Is the destruction of "*all flesh*" going to mean the obliteration of the "Seed" God said would bruise his head?

"*But Noah*" (Genesis 6:8)—let us praise the Lord for this blessed "*but.*" God preserved one who was free from the evil of his day. In fact, if the theory of sexual intercourse existing between the fallen angels and the daughters of men, which brought about such an abominable corruption and made the flood an absolute necessity be true, then the only inference one can draw from the phrase "*Noah...perfect in his generations*" (verse 9) is that both he and his family had preserved their pedigree—pure from Adam.

With the utter destruction of the antediluvians by the flood, God defeated the third attempt of Satan to thwart His redemptive purpose, for in preserving Noah both from the corruption of his age and the judgment falling upon such corruption, God made it possible to continue the Seed of the woman that would yet bruise the serpent's head. And so, reaching Genesis 9, we find God making a fresh start with man upon an earth that had been cleansed and washed of the evil that had stained it by the waters of judgment. Thus the curtain

IN ORDER FOR GOD TO ACCOMPLISH HIS HEAD-BRUISING PROMISE IN GENESIS 3:15, HE SELECTS FROM AMONG THE NATIONS A PEOPLE FOR HIS OWN POSSESSION.

falls upon the first period of human history with its failure on the devil's part to thwart the supreme counsels of the Lord Most High.

THE JEWISH NATION

The Bible contains a wonderful progress of revelation as well as doctrine. Thus, with the opening of Genesis 12, God's gracious scheme of man's deliverance from both sin and Satan begins to crystalize. The mighty river is now entering a narrower channel. After the scattering of Noah's sons, nations increased in number and the earth was replenished, but permeating the life of this new race was a spirit of independence with respect to God. And such a satanic spirit ended in confusion and scattering.

In order for God to accomplish his head-bruising promise in Genesis 3:15, He selects from among the nations a people for His own possession. And it is now our purpose to follow the trail of the serpent as he seeks to circumvent God at every turn of the way with His covenant people, the Jews.

THE FIRST JEW

> *And I will make of thee a great nation, and I will bless thee, and make thy name great; and thou shalt be a blessing: and I will bless them that bless thee, and curse him that curseth thee: and in thee shall all families of the earth be blessed.* (Genesis 12:2–3)

Abraham was the first one to be called a *"Hebrew"* (Genesis 14:13). And it was this first Hebrew who received from God the glorious promise of Genesis 12:2–3, in which both Jew and Gentile can participate.

If the purpose of God is to be frustrated, the devil must have Abraham out of the way, and so he makes two or three attempts to interfere with the patriarch's seed. The first is found in Genesis 12:10–20, where Satan leads Abraham to forsake the place of blessing; and where, had it not been for God's protection, his wife Sarah would have forfeited the right to bear any seed to Abraham. Turning to Genesis 20, we have a similar failure on Abraham's part. But, here again God overrules and Genesis 21 opens with the birth of Isaac, through whom the promise given to Abraham is continued, and from whom Jesus sprang as *"the son of Abraham"* (Matthew 1:1).

Before leaving Abraham and his kindred, we can turn to Genesis 12:6–7 to see another one of Satan's subtle attempts to frustrate God. *"The Canaanite was then in the land."* The promise was *"unto thy seed will I give this land,"* but the aim of Satan was to occupy Canaan in advance of Abraham, in order to contest its occupation by his seed.

THE FIRST FAMILY

Leaving Abraham, head of the Jewish race, as he did in the case of Adam, head of the human race, the devil now turns his attention to the chosen family of Jacob. From Genesis 37–50 unfolds the great messianic purposes of God. The twelve sons of Jacob, who became the representatives of the twelve tribes of the Jewish nation, fill the pages of this part of holy writ.

But in the severe famine covering the face of the earth (see Genesis 41:56), we can detect the next attempt of the "destroyer" to exterminate "the seed of Jacob." And how nearly he succeeded both in the threatened death of young Joseph and in his subsequent trials. That Satan was foiled again can be gleaned from Joseph's word after the revelation of himself to his brethren: *"Ye thought evil against me; but God meant it unto good, to bring to pass, as it is this day, to save much people alive"* (Genesis 50:20). In Genesis 45:5, Joseph also speaks about God sending him ahead to preserve life, which means, as indicated in verse 7, the preserving of posterity in the earth. Hence, the birth of the true Joseph was ensured. He is our *"Zaphnathpaaneah,"* as Joseph was named by Pharaoh in Genesis 41:45—a name meaning "savior of the world."

THE JEWISH NATION

At the opening of Exodus, we are informed that *"the children of Israel* [Jacob's divine name given in Genesis 32:28, meaning "God commands, orders or rules"] *were fruitful, and increased abundantly, and multiplied, and waxed exceeding mighty; and the land was filled with them*" (Exodus 1:7). The Hebrew people are now not merely one family, but have developed into a mighty nation, greater even than the Egyptians. (See Genesis 12:2; Exodus 1:9.) Let us now discover the machinations of Satan as he strives to outwit the redemptive plan of God through this chosen nation.

SATAN'S FIRST ATTEMPT

The "murderer" endeavors, in the first place, to obliterate all the male seed of Israel born in Egypt. What a devilish plan he put into the heart of Egypt's king in Exodus 1:15–16! But notice how wonderfully God defeated such a cruel purpose. Those godly Hebrew midwives were His provision and did not accede to Pharaoh's request. (See Exodus 1:17–20.)

And when this disappointed, jealous-minded, hardhearted ruler took matters into his own hands, there were two saintly souls who, because "*they were not afraid of the king's commandment*" (Hebrews 11:23), hid their child Moses, who became Israel's leader and mediator, both Godward and manward. Let it be noted that the devil overreached, for Pharaoh had to pay for the feeding, clothing, and educating of the goodly child on whom Pharaoh's daughter had compassion. As she discovered him, "*the babe wept*" (Exodus 2:6); and in those tears lay the defeat of the enemy, the preservation of the nation, the faithfulness of Jehovah's word, the destruction of "the wisdom of Egypt," and the coming of the seed of the woman. (See Exodus 1:10; Job 5:12–13.)

SATAN'S SECOND ATTEMPT

But Satan, in his desperation to blot out this chosen nation, is not easily discouraged. When we reach Exodus 14, we find Israel out of the land of Egypt. In verse 11 and 12, however, a bitter complaint is made against Moses. What kind of deliverance was this when before them was the deep sea and behind them the chariots of Pharaoh? Truly it was a crucial moment! Is Satan going to succeed in destroying the chosen nation, either by slaughter or drowning? Israel learned

ISRAEL LEARNED THAT IT WAS A REAL THING TO STAND STILL AND WITNESS THE SALVATION OF THE LORD. NO NATION OR INDIVIDUAL IS ABLE TO FIGHT AGAINST THE DEVIL, NO MATTER THE "PHARAOH" HE USES TO WEAVE HIS WEB.

that day that it was a real thing to stand still (it was all they could do), and witness the salvation of the Lord. No nation or individual is able to fight against the devil, no matter the "Pharaoh" he uses to weave his web. *"The LORD shall fight for you, and ye shall hold your peace"* (Exodus 14:14)—and in the miracle that followed lay Israel's victory and Satan's defeat. Yes, it was God who did it. (See Psalm 106:9–10.)

SATAN'S THIRD ATTEMPT

In the course of time, Israel's form of government changed from a theocracy, one which is God-ruled, to a monarchy, one which is man-ruled. After the death of Moses and Joshua, judges were raised up to guide the affairs of the people. But with the opening of the book of Samuel, the nation is merged into a kingdom, and Israel, like the surrounding nations, has her throne and king. There is one link in the chain of antagonism during the transitional period of Israel's history we can profitably refer to. It is found in the book of Ruth. How disastrous it would have been had Ruth the Moabite returned to Moab along with Orpah, her sister-in-law, when urged to do so by Naomi. Had she gone, she would not have become the wife of Boaz, the mother of Obed, the grandmother of Jesse, the great-grandmother of David, and the ancestress of our blessed Lord. (See Matthew 1:5.)

In coming to the kingdom-phase of Satan's antagonism, we believe that he was aware of Jacob's prophetic utterance in Genesis 49:10: *"The scepter shall not depart from Judah, nor a lawgiver from between his feet, until Shiloh come; and unto him shall the gathering of the people be."* Therefore, we have in this period of the kingdom, the most thrilling and yet hellish means devised by Satan to break God's word. In drastic ways, Satan seeks the destruction of "the Seed Royal" in order to sever the messianic line. We can classify the most prominent assaults of the enemy during the monarchy, united and divided, as follows:

THE ROYAL TRIBE

In 1 Samuel 8:5, we find Israel demanding a king. Such a request is acceded to, but the cunning, skillful enemy does all that he can to transfer the rule or scepter from the tribe of Judah, which, as we have seen from Genesis 49:10, was the line from which the Royal One was to spring. The people chose Saul, who was of the tribe of Benjamin. Saul's name means "asked for." Had the government of Israel remained in Benjamin's tribe, God's promise of Genesis 49:10 would have been perverted. Saul's career clearly demonstrates that the Israelites were moved by Satan to appoint him as king, even as at a later date, he moved David to number Israel. As one writer suggests, Saul is a perfect human understudy of Satan: "There is portrayed for us, with great faithfulness in detail, by the Holy Spirit, the character and career of a man, who fills out with strange exactness, this strange story of Satan. It is found in the biography of King Saul of Israel."[1]

THE ROYAL SEED

With the abandonment of Saul, the throne of Israel is transferred from the tribe of Benjamin to the tribe of Judah. (See 1 Samuel 16.) David, a man after God's own heart, is chosen and anointed king. (See 1 Samuel 16:13; 2 Samuel 2:4; 2 Samuel 5:3.) And with such a change, there commences the desperate and determined attack of Satan upon "the Seed Royal," that is, the house of Judah, from which the Messiah must spring.

Let us follow Satan's evil trail, grouping our material around personalities:

DAVID (1 SAMUEL 18:19)

Saul, the God-forsaken, Satan-possessed monarch (see 1 Samuel 16:14) tries his utmost to destroy the Lord's anointed one, and thus David is obliged to flee as a fugitive, hiding in caves and holds from his father-in-law. Three outstanding attempts were made by Saul to slay David, but this sweet psalmist of Israel could sing, "*He shall reward evil unto mine enemies: cut them off in thy truth. …For he hath delivered me out of all trouble: and mine eye hath seen his desire upon*

1. Samuel Dickey Gordon, *Quiet Talks about the Tempter* (New York: Fleming H. Revell, 1914), 44.

mine enemies" (Psalm 54:5, 7). As we shall see, these three attempts correspond in some measure to the three attempts Satan made to overcome our Lord in the temptations of the wilderness.

Before turning from David's career, however, it may be fitting to observe that he, too, became a tool of Satan. The first mention of Satan in the capacity of an adversary is in 1 Chronicles 21:1: "*Satan stood up against Israel, and provoked David to number Israel.*" No wonder God was "*displeased with this thing*" (1 Chronicles 21:7). Puffed up with pride over the number, David might have gone to war and blotted out the five hundred thousand men of Judah. (See 2 Samuel 24:9.)

JEHORAM (2 CHRONICLES 21:1–17)

In the union of Jehoram and Athaliah, the daughter of Ahab, king of Israel, Satan continues his assault upon the house of Judah. Jehoram slew all his brethren (2 Chronicles 21:4) while he himself died of an incurable disease and "*departed without being desired*" (verse 21:20). Jehoahaz, who is mentioned as Ahaziah in 2 Chronicles 22:1 or Azariah in verse 6, reigned in Jehoram's stead. This ungodly ruler, walking in the evil ways of Athaliah, his mother, is slain along with others of the house of Judah. (See 2 Chronicles 22:8.)

At this critical moment, God's promise appears to be at stake. The Royal Seeds are becoming fewer and fewer. In fact, the light was almost quenched for Athaliah "*arose and destroyed all the seed royal of the house of Judah*" (2 Chronicles 22:10). What followed? "*But Jehoshabeath* [another blessed, divine "*but*" the devil hates], *the daughter of the king, took Joash the son of Ahaziah, and stole him....* [And] *hid him from Athaliah, so that she slew him not*" (verses 11–12). For six years, this cruel-hearted queen reigned over Judah, the self-conscious and apparently sole survivor of the royal house, yet she was not of Judah, but of Israel.

How much depended on the preservation of Joash! If he dies, Judah's light and hope is completely extinguished. Everything depends on this precious child. Carefully, he is hidden and cared for while Athaliah reigns in blissful ignorance, until the day dawns when

WITH THE CONTINUATION OF THE HISTORY OF JUDAH, THERE IS THE CONTINUATION OF THE SATANIC ONSLAUGHT AGAINST THE MESSIANIC SEED WITHIN SUCH A ROYAL LINE.

Joash is presented and crowned as king over Judah and the queen is slain. (See 2 Kings 11:4–12; 2 Chronicles 21:7; 23:11.) Thus, God, in a marvelous way, defeats the evil tactics of the devil, thereby fulfilling the promise of giving a light forever. (See 2 Chronicles 21:7.) In summarizing the mischief of Jehoram's wrongful affinity with Athaliah (see 2 Chronicles 18:1), we can trace the enemy's design in breaking into the royal line so as to destroy the promise of Genesis 3:15 and 2 Samuel 7:16. Jehoshaphat marks the beginning (see 2 Chronicles 18:1); Jehoram follows (see 2 Chronicles 21:4); and the Arabians continue the assault (see 2 Chronicles 21:17; 22:1) as Athaliah nearly succeeds in accomplishing the design of Satan (see 2 Chronicles 22:10).

HEZEKIAH (ISAIAH 36:1; 28:1)

With the continuation of the history of Judah, there is the continuation of the satanic onslaught against the Messianic seed within such a royal line. And so we reach another stage of the age-long conflict in the life and service of good King Hezekiah.

THE FIRST ASSAULT

Satan's first attack is made through the king of Assyria. But Hezekiah, although smitten with fear and sorrow at the boastful taunts of Rabshakeh, *"spread it before the LORD"* (Isaiah 37:14), and God graciously heard his cry and sent forth *"the angel of the LORD"* (verse 36) to smite the Assyrian host. Truly, deliverance from the devil is wholly of the Lord!

THE SECOND ASSAULT

After the attack of the king of Assyria came the assault of terrors, even death. (See Isaiah 38:1.) According to Hebrews 2:14, we learn that Satan *"had the power of death,"* and so, failing to cut off Hezekiah through one monarch, he tries another. Hezekiah, however, turned his face to the wall and prayed, and God, in response to his cry, added fifteen years to his life.

But see how critical the position is. Hezekiah is childless. If death conquers him, who is there to follow him in the line of Judah? He had no heir to the throne, and in his anxiety, he remembers God's word to David in 2 Samuel 7:12–16. Here again, the Lord of life intervenes, and three years after Hezekiah's deliverance from death, a son is born to him, Manasseh by name, who became the worst of Judah's kings, as his father had been the best. (See 2 Kings 21:1.)

THE CAPTIVITY (ESTHER 3:6, 12, 13; 6:1)

Judah, the royal tribe, was taken into captivity by Nebuchadnezzar, king of Babylon, but the book of Esther testifies to God's secret care over His people. Let us continue to follow the assault of Satan against the nation through whom the Seed of the woman was to come.

In seeking the destruction of all the Jews, the devil sought to use Haman, even as he had tried to use Pharaoh in Egypt. In many ways, Haman is a type of the devil. He had power next to the king (see Esther 3:1). And although Satan had great power, Haman could not use that power apart from King Ahasuerus' permission. (See Esther 3:8–9.)

A sleepless night of the king marked the time for divine action. What God used here to rob Ahasuerus of his rest, we do not know. Suffice it to say that God is able to use small things to accomplish His great purpose, as the story of mighty Goliath proved. With the hanging of Haman, who is called, as no other in Scripture, "*the Jews' enemy*" (Esther 3:10), and with the exaltation of Esther, there came the full emancipation of Judah, and with such, the continuation of God's blessed purpose.

Such a dramatic failure on the part of Satan to overthrow the counsels of God concludes the Old Testament phrase of his antagonism. Doubtless, in the restoration of the Jews, and throughout the Maccabean Period of four hundred years or more, stretching from Malachi to Matthew, the "destroyer" was untiring in his efforts to thwart the messianic plan. As the time drew near for the coming of the Messiah, the devil must have increased his evil devices to prevent such a glorious advent, just as his rage will be intensified as the Second Coming of Christ to the earth draws near. But of this we are certain, all his satanic attacks in the period for which we have no biblical revelation was matched by the eternal power of God. If Satan had succeeded in causing the Old Testament Scriptures to close with the word *"curse"* (Malachi 4:6), this was nothing to boast about. As the saying goes, "He who laughs last, laughs longest"— and so the New Testament commences with the name of Jesus Christ, the One who was coming to bear the curse and to destroy the works of the devil.

THE NEW TESTAMENT

The opening of the gospel story with the genealogy of our Lord is of twofold significance. First, we are shown His connection with the line or house of Judah. And for this reason, it is interesting to trace Christ's lineage back to David, as Matthew does, for the question asked by every Jew of anyone who claimed to be the Messiah was, "Is he of the house of David?" And so, both Matthew and Luke mention David in their genealogies.

It may be fitting at this point to add a word or two regarding the difference between these two genealogies as we have them in Matthew 1 and Luke 3. Matthew traces the royal succession, thus proving that Jesus Christ was the Son of David. Luke, on the other hand, gives us the family lineage, and true to the scope of his gospel, traces our Lord's pedigree from the common father of Jew and Gentile, namely, Adam. Matthew differs from Luke in naming women in the genealogy. Of the four referred to, three—Tamar, Rahab, and Bathsheba—were stained with sin. Perhaps the purpose of Matthew in recording such characters is to show that He who came to save the lost did not scorn such descent. As women like these were not excluded from the honor of being in the Messiah's line of ancestry, so others like them would not be shut out from fellowship in His kingdom of grace and love.

For a further insight into the significance of these genealogies, one is referred to a reliable commentary, like *Ellicott's Bible*

Commentary, where it is easy to prove that the names mentioned in the lists preserved the line of Judah from destruction until the emergence of Christ as "the conquering Lion."

The next purpose served by these genealogies is to remind us of Satan's failure to break the direct messianic line stretching from Adam to Christ. These seemingly dry records of names are a testimony to the fact that all the diabolical methods of the enemy to destroy the house of Judah had miserably failed. Apart from the Old Testament characters we have already mentioned, as being specially singled out for satanic assaults, others are mentioned in the genealogies of Matthew and Luke, of which, if we but had the full story of their lives, would be found notable as targets for the devil's anti-messianic darts.

Taking up the threads again of this absorbing theme of Satan's antagonism to "the seed royal," there are two conspicuous periods in which he stands unmasked as the tempter, murderer, liar, prince of demons, adversary, and destroyer.

BEFORE CHRIST'S BIRTH

In his role of accuser, Satan approached Joseph, the husband of Mary, regarding her pregnant condition. A careful study of Matthew 1:18–25 reveals the fact that Joseph's fear was worked on by the devil. Says Ellicott,

> The glimpse given us into the character of Joseph is one of singular tenderness and beauty. To him, conscious of being of the house of David, and cherishing Messianic hopes, what he heard would seem to come as blighting those hopes. He dared not, as a "righteous" man, take to himself one who seemed thus to have sinned. But love and pity alike hindered him from pressing the law, which made death by stoning the punishment of such a sin (see Deuteronomy 22:21), or even from publicly breaking off the marriage on the ground of the apparent guilt. There remained the alternative, which the growing frequency of divorce made easy, of availing himself

> of a "writ of divorcement," which did not necessarily specify the ground of repudiation, except in vague language implying disagreement. (See Matthew 19:3.) Thus the matter would be settled quietly without exposure. The "bill of divorcement" was as necessary for the betrothed as for those who were fully man and wife."[2]

Now, while Joseph *"thought on these things"* (Matthew 1:20), words that suggest conflict or perplexity about such a step, the angel of the Lord came to dissolve his doubts and relieve the anxiety of his mind.

And so the devil failed with this New Testament Joseph, even as he did with his Old Testament namesake. Joseph's pondering was Satan's assault even as he had assaulted Abraham in Genesis 12:11.

AFTER CHRIST'S BIRTH

If ever the demons had a bad day with their satanic monarch, it was on the day that Jesus was *"made of a woman"* (Galatians 4:4). In the promise that her seed would bruise the serpent's head lay the hope that God had set before fallen humanity. And throughout the entire array of those in the Old Testament who had descended from "the woman," Satan had found no one to fear. But here was a marvel—a child, divinely conceived and born, and all at once, the devil's murderous energies are aroused, and his subtle wisdom employed for the slaughter of Mary's infant.

The utter destruction of Satan and all his evil works rested upon One over whom Satan had no control, One who was sinless, both by birth and practice. And that our Lord was holy by birth is proved by the mention of "her seed." Such a thought, as a woman's seed, stated here, is not found elsewhere. Over a hundred times or more, when we read of a seed and seeds, of Abraham's seed, and so forth, it is always *the seed of the man*. But *the seed of the woman* (see Genesis 3:15) is a unique concept and can only be interpreted as a foreshadowing of the

---

2. Charles J. Ellicott, *Ellicott's Bible Commentary: Volume 3* (entry for Matthew 1:19).

THE SEED OF THE WOMAN IS A UNIQUE CONCEPT AND CAN ONLY BE INTERPRETED AS A FORESHADOWING OF THE VIRGIN BIRTH, AND MOST REMARKABLE IT IS THAT IT SHOULD BE FOUND HERE. IF OUR LORD HAD NOT BEEN BORN OF A VIRGIN, IT WOULD HAVE BEEN ADAM AND *HIS SEED* THAT WOULD HAVE BEEN REFERRED TO IN MATTHEW 1:18.

virgin birth, and most remarkable it is that it should be found here. If our Lord had not been born of a virgin, it would have been Adam and *his seed* that would have been referred to in Matthew 1:18. In a very true sense then, the prince of this world had, and consequently found, nothing he could corrupt in the One who sprang from "her seed."

Incidentally, with the coming of Christ, we have a fuller revelation of the cruel machinations of the devil, for no one so scathingly portrayed Satan's hellish character as the Master, who had come to destroy his works. Jesus refers to Satan at least fifteen times under different names, each of which confirms an aspect of Satan's personality. And it was because Christ knew Satan as no other, that with repeated onslaught through many agents, he cruelly opposed Him throughout His earthly life. When Abraham was called, he and his seed were bitterly attacked. After David was enthroned, the royal line was constantly assailed. And when "the seed of the woman" Himself came, the storm burst upon Him. Thus, we come to trace some of the most hellish assaults ever made by the enemy, as a roaring lion against an individual, as well as some of Satan's most cunning devices, as the angel of light, to deceive a trusting soul.

DEPARTURE FROM THE WILL OF GOD

In his endeavor to entice our Lord away from the revealed plan of God for His life, Satan stands unmasked as our Lord's fierce rival. In fact, while the Savior was on earth, there were two protagonists bent on destroying each other's ministry and influence: the devil and one "*stronger than he*" (Luke 11:22). There are at least three phases of this bitter conflict between God's adversary and God's Son:

THE TEMPTATION IN THE WILDERNESS (MATTHEW 4:1–11)

At the very outset of the Master's ministry, He was brought face to face with the devil. Fresh from His divine approval and baptism in the Jordan River, He encountered the diabolical antagonist, who is here named "the devil," for the first time in the Gospels. And if there is no devil, then there is no Christ, for both are represented as speaking to each other. It is not our present purpose to enter into all the details of Satan's daring attempt to make Christ a sinner. A short word on each temptation will suffice.

In the first temptation, to make bread out of stones, it is not difficult to pick up the satanic trail. Satan wanted Christ to assert His own power and thus satisfy a natural need. If He was the Son of God, did not that involve a lordship over nature? Then why not make bread out of the loaf-like stones of the Jordan desert and thereby appease His pangs of hunger? With this first exercise of miraculous power, of which He was the conscious possessor, He would establish His *status* as the Messiah in the eyes of the Jews. But such an expression of His power, although legitimate when hungry crowds must be fed, would have been an act of self-assertion and distrust on the Savior's part, and therefore, would have involved not the affirmation but the denial of Sonship that had so recently been attested. If His Father had given Him a work to do, He would be sustained until its completion.

In the second temptation, Christ is taken to the pinnacle of the temple and told to cast himself down. And in this subtle suggestion, Satan desires Christ to test His attestation that He was the beloved Son. What a crucial experiment of Sonship! By such a sudden appearance in the temple, Christ would obtain power and popularity; and, as to the possibility of destroying himself in descending, had not God promised angelic guardianship? But this attempt to identify Christ with vain-glory, spectacular popularity, and distrust is thwarted by the Savior. The tempter's name is worthy of note at this point. "Devil" is derived from the Greek word *diabolos—dia*, meaning "down" and *bolos* meaning "to throw." Satan is well-named as "thrower-down." Someone has truly said, "The devil *throws down*; the blessed Savior *lifts up*." This second attempt to destroy Christ is foiled.

In the third temptation, Satan's pretensions are very clear. He now addresses his temptation not to the sense of Sonship but to the love of power. To be a king like other kings, mighty to deliver people from their oppressors and to achieve the glory the prophets had predicted for the Messiah, He would need to go beyond the self-imposed limits of accepting whatsoever His Father ordered for Him.

JESUS DID NOT ASK SATAN
TO POLITELY GO;
HE COMMANDED HIM TO RETREAT.
AND THE ENCOURAGING THING FOR
OUR HEART IS THAT SATAN OBEYED.

The purpose of Satan is apparent. He is *"the god of this world"* (2 Corinthians 4:4) and will not allow any relationship to the true God. Satan's attitude of pretense is very often the same as the attitude of a pretender to the throne—he claims it as his right. And that our Lord recognized the devil's right to the kingdom of this world is evident from the fact that three times over He alluded to him as its *"prince"* (John 12:31; 14:30; 16:11), while Paul refers to Satan's hosts as *"the rulers of the darkness of this world"* (Ephesians 6:12). But Satan is a usurper prince, seeing that Christ is *"the prince of the kings of the earth"* (Revelation 1:5), *"the Prince of life"* (Acts 3:15), and *"The Prince of Peace"* (Isaiah 9:6). As crafty Absalom stole the hearts of King David's subjects, so Satan is out to rob God of His own. *"Fall down and worship me"* (Matthew 4:9)—what arrogant assumption and blatant self-importance! What naked and absolute antagonism to the divine will!

Look at Christ's treatment of the tempter at this final stage: *"Get thee hence"* (verse 10). What an assertion of divine power and authority even over the devil! "Leave!" Jesus did not ask him to politely go; He commanded him to retreat. And the encouraging thing for our heart is that Satan obeyed.

Before closing this section of our meditation, it will be found profitable to contrast the two initial assaults of the devil. The first Adam failed to overcome Satan in a garden—the last Adam succeeded. And the circumstances of each tempted one were different. Adam had a wife by his side—Christ was alone. Adam's conflict was in a garden—Christ's was in the wilderness. Adam had plenty around him—Christ was hungry. Adam had safety amid the trees—Christ was surrounded by wild beasts.

May ours be the resolute determination to make our Lord's glorious victory over the devil more actual in our own lives!

THE CLAMOR FOR KINGSHIP (JOHN 6:15)

There may be another evidence of Satan's purpose to sidetrack Christ from His work as Redeemer in this passage, in which the populace, after the miracle of the loaves, sought by force to carry Jesus to the royal city and acclaim Him as their temporal king. But such a shortcut to the throne would have been a direct departure from the will of God, namely, that the Savior was to reach His throne *via* the tree. *"I, if I be lifted up…will draw all men unto me"* (John 12:32). And we have to learn, even as the devil did when Christ, in evading the crowd, turned His back on a crown, that there are no quick, easy steps up to God's throne: *"To him that overcometh will I grant to sit with me in my throne"* (Revelation 3:21).

THE EASIER PATH (MARK 8:31–33)

Here we have another insight into Satan's subtle method of leading Christ into By-Path Meadow [that place in *The Pilgrim's Progress* where one strayed from the narrow path for momentary and fleeting comfort]. Peter is startled as our Lord unfolds many of the terrible experiences ahead to which He would yield, and with impetuous speech, he blurted out, *"Be it far from thee"* (Matthew 16:22). Peter wanted his Lord to gain a kingdom without sacrifice, victory without suffering, a crown without a cross. This warmhearted yet impulsive disciple did not realize that just as God had lifted him up as a trumpet and blown a blast through him regarding Christ's deity, one that Jesus recognized as the voice of the Father, so now Satan is using him to blow a different blast. But Jesus quickly detects the satanic suggestion and identifies Peter's desire to have his Master pity himself with Satan, whose first beginnings of deception are along the line of self-pity.

Notice how Christ meets the tempter. He rebukes Satan as being in Peter: *"But* [Jesus] *turned, and said unto Peter, Get thee behind me, Satan"* (verse 23). The sharpness of the reply indicates a strong and intense emotion. The devil is spoken to by Christ, as he was in the wilderness, for this approach was nothing less than a renewal of the same temptation. He desired Christ to gain His crown without the cross—to draw back from the path the Father had appointed for Him. And so, knowing that Calvary was the only fulfillment of the redemption promise of God in Genesis 3:15, Christ turns from Satan with the stinging rebuke: *"Thou art an offense unto me"* (verse 23).

PREMATURE DEATH

Departure from God or death before the cross—such was the devil's double-barreled gun loaded against Christ. For thousands of years, Satan had laughed at God's redemptive scheme, ridiculing and scorning the hope embodied in the pronouncement in the garden. But God was not upset or alarmed about the final issue. *"It was impossible for God to lie"* (Hebrews 6:18), therefore, in spite of all the efforts of Satan to block his own deserved defeat, Christ came according to promise; and from the moment of His miraculous birth, the destroyer's great passion was to give Christ a speedy exit. As the power of death was still in Satan's hands, he endeavored in various ways to bring the Lord of Life to a premature death. Let us mark several of his murderous approaches.

THE HERODS

If, as we have noted, the Old Testament presents us with fitting types of Satan in Saul and Haman, then, in the New Testament, we also can detect human personifications of the devil's subtlety and cruelty.

1. HEROD THE GREAT (MATTHEW 2:1–23)

There is a certain correspondence between the tactics employed against the promised "seed" in the Old Testament and the actual "Seed" in the New Testament. For example, in the case of Joseph in Matthew 2, there was the crafty work of doubt and suspicion, as in the case of Eve in Genesis 3.

And then, with the introduction of both family and national life, the devil stands out, branded like Cain as a "murderer," for the slaughter of Abel and then of the male children of Israel through Pharaoh was conceived in his murderous heart. And here in the New Testament, Herod becomes the tool of Satan in the cruel massacre of the innocents, the number of which, if the population of Bethlehem

HAD THE INNOCENT BABY JESUS BEEN AMONG THAT LOWLY BAND OF SUFFERERS, WHAT A DARK DAY IT WOULD HAVE BEEN FOR THE WORLD. BUT THE DEVIL DID NOT SUCCEED, FOR JUST AS GOD INTERVENED IN THE SPARING OF MOSES, SO JOSEPH AND MARY, THROUGH THE MEDIUM OF A DREAM, DEFEATED THE CUNNING PLAN OF HEROD, WHICH WAS BUT THE PRODUCT OF SATAN'S CRUEL MIND.

at the time was about two thousand, did not exceed thirty in all. Yes, and let it not be forgotten that the first martyrs for Christ's sake were these precious children of Rachael. Had the innocent baby Jesus been among that lowly band of sufferers, what a dark day it would have been for the world. But the devil did not succeed, for just as God intervened in the sparing of Moses, so Joseph and Mary, through the medium of a dream, defeated the cunning plan of Herod, which was but the product of Satan's cruel mind. Divine interposition was needed to outwit the designs of the enemy; and guidance was given to our Lord's guardians only as and when needed. (See Matthew 2:19–21.)

But further suppose that Christ had been among those dear babies, doomed to die. Herod would not have succeeded, for Mary's helpless babe was the *"mighty God"* (Isaiah 9:6), and as the sinless One, premature death such as the devil planned could have no claim upon Him.

2. HEROD ANTIPAS (LUKE 13:31–35)

"Herod will kill thee" (Luke 13:31)—what startling words these are! Our Lord's answer: *"Go ye, and tell that fox…"* (verse 32) favors the idea that the Pharisees had been sent by this Herod, the son of Herod the Great, to announce his purpose as a threat. It is true that in Luke 23:8, we are told that this self-same Herod was *"desirous to see him of a long season,"* but oscillations of vague curiosity and vague fears were quite in keeping with the tetrarch's character. The answer of Christ is the only word of unmitigated contempt recorded among the utterances of our Lord. And such a reply was more than justified by the mingled tyranny and timidity, insolence and baseness, of Herod Antipas. *"Go ye, and tell that fox."* This word was eminently descriptive of the character of Herod, and of the whole Herodian house. For instance, in the previous Herod, you have the craftiness of the man in the guise of a worshipper of the very one he desired to slay.

Says Ellicott, "The fact that the Greek word for *'fox'* is always used as a feminine, gives, perhaps, a special touch of indignant force to the original. He had so identified himself with his wife, Herodias, that he had lost his manliness, and the proverbial type of the worst form of woman's craft was typical of him."[3]

What courage and fearlessness our blessed Lord displayed! Herod "*hoped to have seen some miracle done by him*" (Luke 23:8). But Jesus gave him no satisfaction, for he had already announced that the time for such sights and wonders was all but over: "*I do cures to day and to morrow, and the third day I shall be perfected*" (Luke 13:32). In effect, our Lord's silent reply to Herod's threat means—"I shall stay in Herod's dominion with perfect security for a brief while longer until my work is done." And walk and work He did until His miraculous ministry was completed with the crowning miracle at Bethany. (See John 11:40–44.)

Poor Herod, he was but the devil's tool! His foxlike character, reflected in the knavish craftiness of the Pharisees, was a gift of Satan. Beyond the desire of Herod to kill Jesus, we can discern the cunning plan of Satan to bring Christ to an untimely end. But into the death-purpose of the devil, Christ flings the word: "*I must walk today, and to morrow, and the day following*" (Luke 13:33). In spite of the devil and his host of demons, Christ as "the King Immortal" was immortal until His work was done.

THE PHARISEES AND JEWISH LEADERS

Christ's age-long antagonist had no more willing confederates in his diabolical purpose to bring our Lord to a speedy end than the Pharisees and Sadducees, who, although it may sound ironic, were the most strictly religious people of Christ's day. Let the following passages stand out in all their grim nakedness:

> *Then assembled together the chief priests, and the scribes, and the elders of the people, unto the palace of the high priest, who was called Caiaphas, and consulted that they might take Jesus by subtilty, and kill him.* (Matthew 26:3–4)

3. Ellicott (entry for Luke 13:32).

> *And the Pharisees went forth, and straightaway took counsel... against him, how they might destroy him.* (Mark 3:6)

> *All they in the synagogue....led him unto the brow of the hill whereon their city was built, that they might cast him down headlong.* (Luke 4:28–29)

> *I know that ye are Abraham's seed; but ye seek to kill me, because my word hath no place in you.* (John 8:37)

> *Then took they up stones to cast at him.*
> (John 8:59; see also 10:31, 39)

What happened as the result of these repeated attempts upon our Lord's life? Why, He appeared to possess a charmed life for He passed through all these murderous intentions, as the Hebrew youths did through the fiery furnace, wonderfully preserved by God. (See Daniel 3:23–28.)

THE STORMS

In the striking narratives of Matthew 8:23–27 and Mark 4:37–41, we are given another sphere of the devil's activity. By the employment of the word *"behold,"* attention is called to another stage of the bitter conflict. As *"the prince of the power of the air"* (Ephesians 2:2), Satan was responsible for whipping up the sea into fury, thus endangering the lives of all within the boat. The fear-stricken disciples did not know that they were wrestling not against wind and storm but against evil forces using such for the death of the sleeping Master. How did Christ meet this satanic assault? The more literal reading of this passage—*"he...rebuked the wind, and said unto the sea, Peace, be still"* (Mark 4:39)—is immensely suggestive: "He said unto the sea, 'Lie down; be muzzled.'" It is the sort of language one uses in speaking to a dog that is misbehaving. If the word be repeated in the sharp peremptory time of command, in which we speak to a dog, it makes the sense yet more intense and real: "Down, sir! Lie down! Shut up!"

"JESUS SAID UNTO THE SEA, 'LIE DOWN; BE MUZZLED.'" IT IS THE SORT OF LANGUAGE ONE USES IN SPEAKING TO A DOG THAT IS MISBEHAVING. IF THE WORD BE REPEATED IN THE SHARP PEREMPTORY TIME OF COMMAND, IN WHICH WE SPEAK TO A DOG, IT MAKES THE SENSE YET MORE INTENSE AND REAL:

"DOWN, SIR! LIE DOWN! SHUT UP!"

And, as the writer we are quoting at this point goes on to say, the whole passage is significant. It is not the sort of language to be used in talking merely to wind and wave, especially by an evenly-poised Man as our Lord was. There is, at once, the recognition of an evil spirit, or a group of them, who had aroused the unusually violent storm.

The language used is recognition of personality. There was someone at work through wind and water. Whoever that might be is ordered down. He obeys. There was a great calm. But the point to mark just now is that Satan's sphere of action includes wind and water as well as the earth. Note why this is the sphere of his activity—because we are here. As he was after Christ, so he is after Christ's, and through us, the dominion of this realm.

THE GETHSEMANE CONFLICT

That the agony in the garden marked a further stage in Satan's antagonism toward Christ is shown in the accounts of Gethsemane. "*This is your hour, and the power of darkness*" (Luke 22:53), declared our Lord as He emerged from the garden. A striking evidence of a satanic assault is seen in the fact that angelic ministration was given as soon as the conflict was over, as it was in the wilderness conflict. (See Luke 22:47.)

Now, why did our Lord sweat great drops of blood? What is the meaning of His cry, "*O my Father, if it be possible, let this cup pass from me*" (Matthew 26:39)? Surely this request did not mean that He was beginning to shrink from the cross, and that He wanted this "*cup*" kept from Him. Had He not already declared His willingness to drink the cup given Him by His Father? And did He not know that Calvary was the climax of His pilgrimage here below; and that for such a death His face was steadfastly set toward Jerusalem? Did He not declare His delight to do the will of God, even though He knew that that "will" was the cross, with all its shame and agony?

What, then, is the explanation of His cry of anguish in Gethsemane? Simply this: overcome with extreme physical weakness and suffering, He wondered whether He could hold out until the cross was reached. His spirit was willing to tread every inch of the blood-red way to Calvary, but His flesh was so weak. His soul was "crushed with anguish to the very point of death,"[4] as Dr. Weymouth translates Matthew 26:38; and so the phrase from verse 41 we misapply to ourselves is identified with Christ: "My spirit…My flesh."

Having the power of death, it was Satan's passion to get Christ out of the way before the cross. Previous attempts had failed, as we have seen. Is he to succeed in the garden? No, the cup of physical weakness was taken from Him, for an angel came and strengthened the Savior; and rising from the blood-stained dust, He passes away a victor over the foe. Christ emerged from the garden miraculously empowered for the final onslaught. He has one death to die—the death of the cross.

CALVARY

While it is perfectly true that the devil was indirectly responsible for the death of Christ, seeing that He was bearing the curse pronounced upon man for his disobedience in listening to the satanic voice—yet, directly, the devil tried his utmost to prevent Jesus from going to the cross, seeing that His death thereon was the fulfillment of the redemptive promise and prophecy of Genesis 3:15, and also the death-knell of the devil and his works. "*Through death he might destroy him that had the power of death, that is, the devil*" (Hebrews 2:14). And such a death was the last thing Satan desired. He was anxious for Christ to die *before* the cross—not *on* the cross. This death differed from all other deaths. Others *suffer* death; Christ *achieved* it.

To others, death comes to frustrate their work. Christ's death consummated, crowned, and completed His work. It was on the cross that He uttered that triumphant cry, "*It is finished*" (John 19:30). The death of Christ was His greatest work, His supreme act, His most glorious achievement! Hence, the devil's purpose was to block and prevent it.

---

4. Richard Francis Weymouth, *The New Testament in Modern Speech* (1915), 83.

THE JEWS HAVE A LEGEND THAT SATAN ACCUSES MEN DAY AND NIGHT, THE WHOLE YEAR-ROUND, *EXCEPT* ON THE DAY OF ATONEMENT, AND THEN HE IS UTTERLY SILENCED. SURELY THIS TESTIFIES TO WHAT THE ENEMY THINKS OF THE CROSS!

The Jews have a legend that Satan accuses men day and night, the whole year-round, *except* on the Day of Atonement, and then he is utterly silenced. Surely this testifies to what the enemy thinks of the cross!

And that God's adversary and ours did not want Christ to stay on His cross, and utter, not as a poor, emaciated man with a weak, failing voice, but as a mighty Victor conscious of achieving an eternal conquest over all satanic forces, the cry *"It is finished"* can be proved by the fact that Satan sought every possible way to persuade Christ to leave His cross. Read the accounts of the crucifixion and you will find that the rulers, priests, people, and the thieves, all alike, urged Christ to come down from the tree and save himself. But a Christ without His cross is unthinkable. Both have been eternally nailed together.

Behind such pleading voices, there can be detected both the desperation and subtlety of Satan. Had Jesus exercised His own power, and descended, we should have been of all men most miserable. But, marvel of marvels, He stayed there! Hallelujah, what a Savior! And the glory of the gospel is wrapped up in this sublime truth: that poor and weak though we be in ourselves, and no match whatsoever for the devil, we yet have the prerogative of overcoming him through the blood of the Lamb. And let it never be forgotten that Christ refused the myrrh that could have deadened the consciousness of His anguish. He determined to die sublimely conscious that He was a glorious Victor, not a poor emaciated victim. Calvary was to be the devil's Waterloo—and he knew, and knows, it!

THE GRAVE

For Satan's next move, we turn to Matthew 27:62–66. Christ has died and is buried. And if the adversary could not prevent Him from dying on the cross, then he must endeavor to keep Him dead, seeing that His resurrection would be but God's receipt for the debt paid at Calvary. Having a faint knowledge of the far-reaching influence of the resurrection, Satan makes his last great attempt to destroy God's magnificent and perfect plan of redemption. And so, the sepulcher is made sure, the stone sealed, and a watch or guard set. No doubt, all the empire of Satan rang with triumphant shouts, peal on peal, as the spirit of Jesus passed out of His body into paradise. But little did they realize that in His death and burial, Christ had passed right out of Satan's power. The devil knew it only too well.

Yes, and those who thirsted for the blood of Christ might have said,

> Now he is dead! For hence He lies
> In the lorn Syrian town;
> And on his grave, with shining eyes,
> The Syrian stars look down.[5]
> But the Christian's song is of a different strain: "Death cannot keep his prey."[6]

On the third day, the tomb was emptied of the dead body and our Lord arose "a victor from the dark domain."[7] The devil's attempt to keep Christ's body sealed in a tomb was defeated.

Then followed the other half of this last assault against the Lord's Anointed. When the chief priests learned the news of Christ's resurrection, they resorted to a lie, for the soldiers who kept guard were bribed to say that His disciples had come by night and stolen His body. And in their blindness, the soldiers failed to see that such a concocted story was a bad testimony in respect to their vigilance. Anyhow, the lie caught on and was believed among the Jews. (See Matthew 28:15.)

Our Lord declared in the day of His flesh that the devil was a liar: *"For he is a liar, and the father of it"* (John 8:44). True to his character, Satan scattered their fabrication about the empty tomb.

THE RESURRECTION

"Whom God hath raised up [and this the devil knew full well as did also the five hundred brethren]...*it was not possible that he should*

---

5. Poem by Matthew Arnold, "Obermann Once More," 1867.
6. Hymn by Robert Lowry, "Low in the Grave He Lay," 1874.
7. Ibid.

be holden of it" (Acts 2:24). Why not possible? Because He was God as well as man. Because He trusted His Father to raise Him up. Because the Scripture cannot be broken. Because it is unthinkable that the devil and death triumph.

Yes, and not only did He rise again, as He said He would, but He also ascended up on high. (See Acts 1:1–11.) And in His ascension, He passed triumphantly through the realm of "the spiritual hosts of evil, arrayed against us in the heavenly warfare."[8] Having ascended above *"the prince of the power of the air,"* He now makes over to His blood-washed ones the blood-bought victory of Calvary over all the wiles of the devil. "Like another Joash, He is seated and expecting, hidden in the house of God on high; and the members of 'the one body' are hidden there 'in Him' (Hebrews 10:12–13; Colossians 3:1-3). Like another Jehoshaba; and going forth to witness of His coming like another Jehoiada (2 Chronicles 23:3)."[9]

We have reached the end of the second round in this grim contest between Satan and God, hell and heaven, darkness and light, and the Lord Jesus Christ is still the victorious One. In the Old Testament, Satan tried to prevent the "Seed" from coming. In the Gospels, he tried to prevent the "Seed" from living—and when dead, from rising—but God compassed His Son about with songs of deliverance. And now, as the triumphant Lord, He can comfort our devil-beset hearts with the words: *"Fear not; I am the first and the last: I am he that liveth, and was dead; and, behold, I am alive for evermore, Amen; and have the keys of hell and of death"* (Revelation 1:17–18).

---

8. Weymouth, 472.
9. E. W. Bullinger, *The Companion Bible* (1909–1922), appendixes.

PART II

DURING THE CHURCH PERIOD

Cognizant of the fact that Christ had promised to build His church, Satan continues his age-long antagonism. Having failed to destroy Christ, every effort must be made to annihilate what Christ came to produce. The reason, therefore, of Satan's unabated hatred and opposition to the corporate church, and to the individual member of such, was his desire to injure Christ through His church.

Because the church was brought into being to continue the redemptive ministry of her risen and glorified Head, she must be disposed of in some way or another. Her message must be nullified and her witness made of no effect. Thus, in this church age, Satan is striving to thwart and destroy the influence of Christ and Christian teaching through the church. In spite of the fact that Christ declared that the gates of hell can never prevail against His church, the devil yet works untiringly for her overthrow. (See Matthew 16:18.) And the reason of his unabated hatred and opposition is two-fold.

THE MIRACLE OF REGENERATION

It may be that Satan strove to keep Jesus from the cross, seeing that he possibly knew that Calvary would result in Pentecost. By the Holy Spirit, in the work of regeneration, we are made partakers of Christ and of His divine nature. And being indwelt by Christ, the conflict is transferred from Christ to us.

ONCE SAUL'S EYES WERE OPENED TO THE REALITY OF THE POWER OF HELL, HIS GIFTED PEN NEVER RESTED UNTIL, BY MEANS OF HIS LETTERS, HE THOROUGHLY UNMASKED THE DIABOLICAL DESIGNS OF SATAN.

In our unregenerate state, there was no antagonism. Satan was our god, and being under his sway, we encountered no opposition. Being born anew, however, meant that we were immediately brought into contact with heavenly forces and made to realize that such would be opposed by hellish powers.

THE MINISTRY OF RECONCILIATION

In the days of the early church, Satan made a desperate bid to strike at Christ, the Head, through Christians, the members of His body. Thus, as Satan moved David to number Israel, in like manner, he moved Saul of Tarsus to slay all those proclaiming the name of Christ. With authoritative letters from Damascus, Saul, *"breathing out threatenings and slaughter against the disciples"* (Acts 9:1), whether they were men or women, determined to stamp out all who were of Christ, the Way. (See Acts 8:1–5.)

And that Saul of Tarsus, unconsciously, was attacking Christ through His disciples is clearly seen in our Lord's reply to Saul's question, *"Who art thou, Lord?"*: *"I am Jesus whom thou persecutest"* (Acts 9:5). The proposed slaughter of the disciples was really a blow struck at Christ. Through Saul, Satan was seeking to wipe out the testimony of the cross and the resurrection, knowing that the preaching of such events would cause his kingdom to totter in many a life. Over five hundred brethren had seen the risen Lord, and every effort had to be made to exterminate them; hence Satan's inspiration of Saul in his passion to slaughter the disciples.

The Lord, however, not only rules but overrules. He can make the wrath of man to praise Him, as is evident by Saul's conversion. Once the tool of the enemy, Saul, soon to become Paul, lived to become the greatest opponent, next to Christ, the devil has ever had. Once Saul's eyes were opened to the reality of the power of hell, his gifted pen never rested until, by means of his letters, he thoroughly unmasked the diabolical designs of Satan. The mighty labors of the apostle Paul must have produced constant anger in the courts of his satanic majesty. And this was the man who, in spite of demons and men, could lay down his task, confident that he had kept the faith.

THE EARLY CHURCH

The Acts of the Apostles and the epistles are not only records of what the Holy Spirit made possible through the apostles, they also contain a valuable contribution to Satan's record as the cruel antagonist of Christ and His own. Let us enumerate some of the methods he adopted to ruin the testimony of the church in the early days of her existence.

SEVERE PERSECUTION

Commencing with Saul's ambition to slaughter the disciples, Satan appears to have been tremendously active in the days when the church had power to turn the world upside down.

What battles for the Lord those early disciples had to wage! What terrible persecutions were theirs! A volume like *The Catacombs of Rome* reveals the horrible ways by which the devil, as murderer, sought to exterminate the saints. Many perished for Christ's sake; but, as ever, the blood of the martyrs is the seed of the church. Thus, in spite of the rage of hell, the testimony goes on.

HINDERED SERVICE

A close study of Paul's epistles convinces one of Satan's realities as a person. To the apostle, Satan was not only an evil force, but a personality—subtle, cruel, and persistent. And it is Paul who acquaints us of the fact that one of the clever disguises of Satan is that of a hinderer. No matter what outward circumstances were preventing the apostle from visiting the Thessalonians, he knew that Satan had hindered him. (See 1 Thessalonians 2:18.)

Great doors of opportunity confronted Paul, but with them, there was also the adversary. Conflicts with men were his, but Paul knew that his seen foes were only the tools of the unseen arch foe. Did he not confess that he wrestled not merely against flesh and blood, but against Satan and his wicked host? (See Ephesians 6:12.)

Being the greatest exponent of Christ and His gospel the church has ever known, all hell would have gone on holiday if Paul had remained blind or been killed in the early days of his witness.

FALSE TEACHING

A casual reading of the epistles, Pauline and general, reveal how Satan tried to wreck the testimony and influence of the church through the propagation of false teaching. Wolves in sheep's clothing sought to harry the flock. Men arose who mixed truth with error. They departed from the faith, turned to fables, and denied the Lord who had brought them. Paul, the wonderful founder of churches, came to the end of his days a broken-hearted man as he viewed the ravages of Satan in some churches he had been used of the Lord to create. Realizing that after his departure, professing Christian men would arise to proclaim a gospel other than the one he had so faithfully preached, he ceased not to warn the flock, and that with tears, of the coming apostasy.

UNHOLY LIVING

As there is nothing that can ruin the influence of the gospel like the inconsistency of those who have embraced it, Satan leaves no stone unturned in his endeavors to sidetrack the saints. And what tragedies he is responsible for! What a poignant passage that is in the Philippian letter, in which Paul speaks of those who once walked by the same rule, but whose earthliness cost him so many tears. Once professed friends, they had become enemies of the cross of Christ. (See Philippians 3:17–19.)

The devil knows, only too well, that sin or worldliness in the life of a believer stabs Christ in the back. As the embodiment of evil, Satan hates holiness and seeks thereby to cripple the cause of Christ through unsanctified living. A holy life is Christ's most powerful weapon against the evil one and all unholy forces.

PHYSICAL WEAKNESS

In the flesh, Jesus was active and fruitful in His resistance of the devil. And it was the Holy Spirit who, occupying the body of our

ONCE SATAN SUCCEEDS IN INCAPACITATING THE MIND OR BODY, HE HAS SET IN MOTION THOSE INFLUENCES DESTRUCTIVE TO A SPIRIT-INSPIRED WITNESS.

Lord, made it the medium of defeat for the devil, and of blessing for his dupes. Apart from weariness, physical weaknesses afflicting our bodies had no place in Jesus's sinless body.

In the story of the woman loosed from her infirmity, Jesus teaches us to believe that Satan was responsible for this woman's physical misery and bondage: "*This woman...whom Satan hath bound, lo, these eighteen years*" (Luke 13:16). Paul, likewise, referred to his physical disability as a messenger of Satan to buffet him. (See 2 Corinthians 12:7.) If Satan can get at our bodies, and, in the old nature he has a vantage point from which to work, then we can expect him to attempt to incapacitate us for service in some way or another. Of course, there are times when sickness is permitted by God, that He might be glorified. Saints, however, through lack of care and forgetful of the fact that the body is the temple and channel of the Holy Spirit, often lay themselves open to the attack of the devil along the avenue of the physical. And once Satan succeeds in incapacitating the mind or body, he has set in motion those influences destructive to a spirit-inspired witness.

THE PRESENT-DAY CHURCH

With church history as our guide, we can travel from the days of the early fathers to the dark, Middle Ages with their terrible persecutions in the name of religion, and from such to the present time, as we mark the slimy trail of the serpent. Let us look at things as they are in order to discover if Satan's hostility toward Christ and His church is as fierce as ever. Has time mellowed him? Have the setbacks he has experienced robbed him of his sting? Has he changed? Not a bit of it! He is just as much a devil as ever he was.

Yes, and a devil he must remain. The saints are to have a new name—not so the devil. His name and diabolical nature are as deathless as himself. His tactics may change, and they do with each succeeding generation, but Satan himself cannot change.

If anything, he is worse now than ever he was. Having an idea of prophecy, he knows that his time is short, and with accelerated speed, he is pursuing his deadly task. Marshalling all his demonic forces together, as he is, for a final onslaught against Christ and His anointed, we can expect intense antagonism in this, our day and generation.

MODERN HERESIES

Paul proves that Satan can be a very religious devil when he writes about the devil transforming himself into *"an angel of light"* (2 Corinthians 11:14). And his manifestation we have to face is not the gruesome representation of a pitchfork-wielding person with horns and tail, but a religious Satanism so subtle and disastrous in its working.

For more than one hundred years, professors and teachers in centers of theological training have had Satan's special attention, and so successful has he been that modernism has thoroughly permeated the church. His ministers—yes, the devil's ministers, for he has many in the ministry—are masquerading as ministers of truth and righteousness.

Modernism, we hold, is the creation of hell, no matter how religious it may be. Modern heresies and criticism are pitted against the infallible Word, the infallible Christ, the fact of sin, the redemptive work of the cross, and the witness of the Holy Spirit. Knowing how completely the deity and death of Christ destroyed his works, Satan, through religious teachers, has been attacking the doctrines of the virgin birth, sinlessness, and efficacious death and resurrection of our blessed Lord. Modernists have taken away our Lord and we know not where they have laid Him.

By modernism, Satan has succeeded in robbing the church of her power in the world. With a humanized Christ, a mutilated Bible, and a glorified self, modernism becomes bankrupt of spiritual power. Nothing can damn evangelism like modernism, and Satan knows it; hence, his untiring efforts to create an ever-increasing army of false teachers. Let us pray for spiritual perception whereby we can detect, and that immediately, the subtle error in a good deal that we hear from some of the pulpits of our land.

MODERN DIVISIONS

Satan has ever been the destroyer of unity. He ruined it among angels; hence, his fall and the casting out of those who took his side. He severed the harmony between God and man; hence, the fall of Adam. He blasted the communion existing between man and man; hence, the slaughter of Abel by Cain.

And the disintegration within the church, from the time of its inception, had its birth in Satan's evil heart. He has ever been conscious of the fact that the mystical union binding believers to the Lord can never be broken. But mutual communion can be severed, as, alas, it is. One has said that *God* made the church; *man* made denominations. But we would like to know how far man was inspired by Satan in such creations. What schisms, bitter feuds, estrangements, splits, and divisions we have, all in the name of denominationalism or nondenominationalism.

We maintain that, in these last days, the present tragic disintegration of Christian forces is Satan's masterpiece to destroy the witness and testimony the church should have. It is his attack at her Head. Being the Lord's creation *"by water and blood"* (1 John 5:6) and destined to function as His representative in the world, the church has ever been hated by the devil. If, therefore, he can succeed in getting her members to fight against each other instead of fighting together against a common foe, then he succeeds in limiting the application of our Lord's redemptive work to a lost world, work that is ever destructive to Satan's power and dominion. And, alas, Christians ignorant of Satan's devices have allowed him to secure an advantage over them by the divisions in the ranks that he himself is originally responsible for. (See 1 Corinthians 1:10–14; 12:25.)

Before leaving this point, it will be remembered that the devil has ever preserved unity among his infernal hosts. Splits, divisions, rebellions never seem to divide his flock. The hellish foes of Christ

THE DEVIL HAS EVER PRESERVED UNITY AMONG HIS INFERNAL HOSTS. SPLITS, DIVISIONS, REBELLIONS NEVER SEEM TO DIVIDE HIS FLOCK. THE HELLISH FOES OF CHRIST AND HIS CHURCH SWEAR CONSTANT ALLEGIANCE TO THEIR PRINCE AND ARE ONE IN THE COVENANT OF DESTRUCTION OF ALL THAT IS SPIRITUAL.

and His church swear constant allegiance to their prince and are one in the covenant of destruction of all that is spiritual. Satan never casts out Satan! (See Matthew 12:26.) The church, however, ravaged by his attacks upon her, is torn asunder by schisms and consequently destitute of authority in the world. May the prayer of her glorious Head be speedily answered: *"That they...may be one"* (John 17:21).

MODERN UNBELIEF

Modernism is guilty of *disbelief*. Unbelief, or *non-belief*, however, characterizes a godless world. To those who are lost in their sin, the gospel is hidden, or veiled. Satan, the god of this world, has *"blinded the minds of them which believe not"* (2 Corinthians 4:4). He resorts to all kinds of means to keep the souls of men in total darkness regarding the true nature of the glorious gospel of Christ.

And the number of those who sit in darkness is colossal. One is nearly cast down in despair to think of the millions Satan is robbing of the Savior. We have lived to see the day of tremendous apathy regarding spiritual things. So-called Christian lands are becoming more pagan with the passing days. There is a great sweep of anti-religious forces all over the world. Worldliness has swamped our communal home, and religious life.

Christian work was never as hard as it is in this carnally-minded age. Blindly, the multitudes are rushing on toward a lost eternity. Drunk with the wine of pleasure, they fail to realize what a rude awakening will be theirs, when, in hell, with a grinning devil over them to mock their moans, they will realize all too late that the door of mercy is closed. Oh, that man could come to learn the cruel heartlessness of Satan as he strives to rob Christ of souls, and souls of Christ! May ours be the Spirit-empowered ministry arousing men and women to the devices of Satan!

MODERN DESTRUCTIONS

It would seem as though Satan is two-faced in this age. He has a sort of Dr. Jekyll-and-Mr. Hyde existence. *"The angel of light"* is the mask covering his face as the *"roaring lion"* (1 Peter 5:8). But no matter how angelic he may appear to be, through all his activities, one increasing purpose is in his heart: murder! A murderer from the beginning, he has ever remained a monster of destruction and death.

Now, these are days of increased gospel activity, both at home and abroad. Think of the way in which mass communications are helping to bring the gospel to millions! And the world has never been flooded with so many Bibles and with Christian literature as it is today. But, with such, there is increased satanic activity. Urged on by his own murderous heart, the devil is out to destroy as many as he can before they have a chance of turning to the Savior.

Conscious of his own final doom, and that there is no salvation whatsoever in store for him, Satan is working with feverish haste to crowd the caverns of the doomed. And truly, his sickle of death is never idle. Think of all the warfare that has slain millions! Think of the bloody revolutions within the last century! Think of the hundreds of thousands who are being killed every year on the streets of our planet!

Yes, and let us make no mistake, we, too, will be open to his murderous attacks, if resisting him, if we yet dare to stand up and confess to a devil-driven world that there is deliverance from Satan's cruel bondage. If we are Spirit-filled, the emissaries of hell will contrive to shorten our days; but we are ever safe in Christ's hand, for no satanic shaft can hit until the Son of God sees fit. Hallelujah!

PART III

AFTER THE CHURCH PERIOD

We have now reached a further, yet final stage in the bitter antagonism of the archenemy of God and man. With superb generalship, Satan is to marshal his hordes together for a decisive conflict. Knowing his time is short, the devil is to manifest great wrath. And woe to those inhabiting the earth when the devil and his hosts are loose among them!

Having failed to annihilate "The Seed" in the Old Testament, to destroy Christ in His day, and to prevail against the true church in her age, Satan now concentrates his attention on the multitudes left behind at the translation of the church.

With the removal of the church, the earth will witness the culmination of anti-Christian forces controlled by the human agent the apostle John identifies as "the antichrist." (See 1 John 2:18, 22; 4:3; 2 John 1:7.) This impersonator of God, personally inspired and indwelt by Satan, the antichrist of all antichrists, will be a terror to all living during the tribulation period.

Perhaps the devil's greatest work at the commencement of this period will be the denial of the miracle of the church's translation, and the beguiling of souls through counterfeit miracles. He will do his utmost to thwart the influences of the rapture just as he labored to nullify the power of Christ's resurrection.

Any display of God's power has always called forth the wrath of the devil. The miraculous birth of Christ was answered by the murder of the innocents by Herod; the benediction of the Father at the River Jordan was met by the fierce temptation of the wilderness; the coming of the Spirit at Pentecost was the occasion of extreme persecution. Outbursts of revival in the church's history have ever been followed by greater activity on the part of Satan. And here, with the glorious miracle of the church's translation, all hell is moved to counteract the influence of such a stupendous display of God's power and grace.

DURING THE TRIBULATION

The concluding book of the Bible was rightly placed in such a divine library. It records the consummation of all things, even of the devil and his works, hence, his hatred of the book of Revelation and his subtlety in keeping people from studying it.

What a book of conflicts it is! It carries the clash of arms all through its pages. Within it, the stage is set for the greatest drama of all ages. Tearing off all disguises, Satan is open and avowed in his antagonism, and prepared for a spectacular overthrow of Christ and His anointed. Briefly, then, let us trace the climax of the conflict of the ages we have been trying to depict in these pages.

For the first half of the tribulation, Satan tries to win the kingdom by flatteries. He enters as peaceably and religiously as he can when occasion demands it. He inspires his agent—the human antichrist—to set himself up in the place of God *as God*. Gradually, however, his real nature is revealed and he stands out as the enemy of the Lord, and of His ancient people, the Jews.

Two avenues of Satan's hate and power are before us in this tragic period, namely the reign of the human antichrist, who represents a vast apostate civil and political power; and the ministry of the false prophet, who functions as the head of religious apostasy. So Christ's right to govern the world is challenged by the antichrist, and Christ's right to the worship of His own is challenged by the false prophet.

At the end of this period, however, Christ descends to earth, and, routing His foes, hellish and human, takes unto Himself His power and reigns. And the description given of the carnage produced by such a conflict is indeed terrible and should lead us to praise God anew that we shall be away from the earth when it transpires.

AFTER THE TRIBULATION

We frankly admit that the book of Revelation contains symbolic language that can be difficult to understand. Still, it was meant to be read, and a special blessing is promised to those who study the book. (See Revelation 1:3.) Neglect of it, however, is general among Christians, and such negligence is produced by the devil, seeing that the book records his own doom.

> [Jesus] *cast* [Satan] *into the bottomless pit, and shut him up, and set a seal upon him, that he should deceive the nations no more, till the thousand years should be fulfilled: and after that he must be loosed a little season.* (Revelation 20:3)

With the setting up of His kingdom, Christ commits Satan to the bottomless pit for a thousand years. What a relief for a sin-cursed, war-scarred earth! Think of it! In a world without a devil, Christ is in supreme control and reigns from shore to shore. For a millennium, He has undisputed sway.

As to the devil, he cannot manifest his antagonism, seeing he is in his prison and has no power to emerge out of his sealed abyss. What irony there is in the phrase "*set a seal upon him*"! Upon the prison of Christ's sepulcher, a seal was set declaring that Satan would not rise. When Christ was crucified and in death's prison, the hymn proclaims the power of resurrection: "He tore the bars away, Jesus, my Lord."[10] Satan's abode is sealed but, alas for him, he has no power to rise. He is detained during His Majesty's pleasure. A "greater power" than he has prevailed and sent him to the abyss.

10. "Christ Arose," hymn by Robert Lowry (1874).

IN A WORLD WITHOUT A DEVIL, CHRIST IS IN SUPREME CONTROL AND REIGNS FROM SHORE TO SHORE. FOR A MILLENNIUM, HE HAS UNDISPUTED SWAY.

PERSONAL ACTIVITY FOR A LITTLE SEASON

At the end of the thousand years, Satan is allowed to leave his prison, and by his deception of the nations, proves that even a millennium in which to reflect and repent works no change in his diabolical nature. The stored-up rage of a thousand years is vomited out upon Christ, and the multitudes He reigns over in peace and righteousness. Gathering the deceived nations together, Satan enters his final conflict. What a blessing it is to know that Satan is only loosed for *"a little season"* (Revelation 20:3)! But released he is, to show that he is still a devil.

One may wonder why so many on earth follow Satan, even after the glorious benefits of Christ's personal reign. With all peace and felicity of such a kingdom, surely Satan will have to fight his concluding battle alone. It must not be forgotten, however, that multitudes only yield feigned obedience to Christ during the millennium. Although Satan is imprisoned in the bottomless pit, the satanic spirit is still imprisoned in many hearts and finds expression as soon as the cruel master is released.

We have no account of the demons being cast into prison along with their prince. During the millennium, many of them are at large and, doubtless, are active in the minds of thousands. Open hostility, however, is impossible owing to Christ's complete control of all things.

PERSONAL SUBJECTIVITY FOREVER

With the setting up of the great white throne, we reach the final subjugation of Satan. The mills of God may grind slowly but they grind exceeding sure. Christ, the Seed of the woman Satan tried to destroy, was manifested that He might destroy the works of the devil. At Calvary, he was virtually deposed, and now, gathering together the fruits of redemptive work, Christ disposes of His satanic foe once and for all.

> *The devil that deceived them was cast into the lake of fire and brimstone, where the beast and the false prophet are, and shall be tormented day and night for ever and ever.* (Revelation 20:10)

What an end for an angelic being once having high rank in the courts of heaven! Behold how the mighty are fallen! The history of this Lucifer can be briefly traced. Once in heaven, he was deposed and cast out into the air. From the air he comes to earth. Then comes the bottomless pit, and after such, the earth again, which, in turn is followed by his sojourn in the lake of fire and brimstone "*for ever and ever.*"

At last, Christ is absolutely supreme. All enemies are under His feet. Satan and sin are finally banished and a new creation is presented to the Father who becomes all in all.

> *And when all things shall be subdued unto him, then shall the Son also himself be subject unto him that put all things under him, that God may be all in all.* (1 Corinthians 15:28)

The earth and the heaven, we are told, flee away from Christ as He sits upon His august throne. (See Revelation 20:11.) *Why the earth?* Because for millennia, it was cursed by sin and came to bear the stain of the Redeemer's blood. So a new earth is provided into which Satan, sin, sorrow, and, separation can never enter. *Why the heavens?* Because they had been polluted by Satan's presence as the prince of the power of the air. Such heavenly spheres could never be clean in the Lord's sight, thus, they give place to heavens as pure as the One creating them.

THE WEAPONS OF OUR WARFARE

The conclusion of the whole matter we have been considering is that we must understand how to use our weapons of warfare, so that, as we tarry amid the shadows of a satanically-controlled world, we may be more than conquerors.

THE WEAPONS OF THE WORLD ARE OF NO AVAIL IN SUCH A CONFLICT WITH THE POWERS OF DARKNESS. WE MUST HAVE MORE DIVINE, MORE SPIRITUAL, MORE CELESTIAL AIDS. AND WE HAVE THEM IN HIM WHO IS OUR *JEHOVAH NISSI*—THE LORD OF HOSTS, OUR BANNER.

It would be blessed indeed if God took us immediately to His heavenly house, but He never does. He leaves us in a world filled with temptation and sin. We have to move through the heart of the enemy's country, and a thousand solicitations from within and without would have us yield to the foe.

And the weapons of the world are of no avail in such a conflict with the powers of darkness. We must have more divine, more spiritual, more celestial aids. And we have them in Him who is our *Jehovah Nissi*—the Lord of hosts, our Banner. He has made every provision for us to be delivered from the pomp and power of the enemy, from the subtle craft and poisonous sweetness of the tempter.

THE WEAPON OF THE WORD

The Word of God, Paul reminds us, is the sword of the Spirit—and a very effective sword it is when wielded against Satan. It was with this weapon that our Lord defeated the enemy as he tempted Him in the wilderness. And if we are to be victorious as we wield the Spirit's sword, we must have more than a mere intelligent conception of the contents of the Bible. Ours must be a living experience of its power.

And one reason why Satan has tried to destroy faith and confidence in the Bible as the inspired Word of God is because he knows, only too well, its effectiveness as a weapon when used against him.

THE WEAPON OF THE BLOOD

As the accuser, the devil can be overcome by the blood of the Lamb. (See Revelation 12:11.) In hours of temptation, the blood ever avails as we plead its efficacy. Satan is a defeated foe and such a defeat can be actualized in our lives as we seek the shelter of the blood. May we learn how to bring the work of the cross to bear on all the wiles and machinations of the enemy!

THE WEAPON OF RESISTANCE

Scripture affirms that if we resist the devil, he will flee from us. (See James 4:7.) We have the prerogative of saying, with the Master,

"Get thee behind me, Satan" (Matthew 16:23)! Because he is neither omnipotent, omnipresent, omniscient, or sovereign, we can overcome him as we resist him in the victory of our omnipotent, omnipresent, omniscient, and sovereign Lord.

Had our Lord been merely man, He could not have had power over the devil and demons; but, being the Son of God, with power, He could exercise authority, even in the region of hell. It is this power, which in virtue of His cross, resurrection, ascension, and gift of the Holy Spirit, He shares with His believing people. May ours be the grace of appropriation!

THE WEAPON OF VIGILANCE

With His disciples, we are exhorted to *"watch and pray"* (Matthew 26:41; see also Mark 14:38), lest we enter into temptation. To *"watch and pray"* means to have one eye on the devil and the other eye on the Lord for deliverance.

> Principalities and powers,
> Mustering their unseen array,
> Wait for thy unguarded hour:
> Watch and pray.[11]

A legend goes as follows:

> Satan held a high and mighty conclave in hell to receive the reports of his evil angels' work. Presently in the assembly a fiend arose and said, "I saw a caravan of Christians crossing the desert, and I raised the terrible simoom [sandstorm], and destroyed them all." "What of that?" replied his master [Satan]; "their souls were all saved."
>
> Then another arising, said, "I saw a ship conveying missionaries and their band of workers to another clime, and I let loose upon them the winds of heaven, and they sank into

11. "Christian! Seek Not Yet Repose," hymn by Charlotte Elliott and William H. Monk (words 1836, music 1868).

> a watery grave." "What of that?" replied the tempter; "their souls were all saved."
>
> There was a moment's pause in the ghastly company, and then another hellish spirit arose and hissed, "I tried for seven years to send a Christian to sleep; and at last I succeeded." "You have done well," returned the evil one; and the vaults of the abyss rang with plaudits and fiendish laughter.[12]

Beloved, it is not fiction that Satan laughs when Christians sleep. Lulled to sleep on the lap of some Delilah, a Christian will work more harm than a thousand worldlings. Without prayer and care, we aid the devil in his work of deceit and destruction. Let us not sleep as do others, but let us watch and be sober.

Vigilant we must be, seeing that the devourer is abroad destroying souls. We must awake the sinner, lest he sleep the sleep that knows no waking till the trump of doom arouses him. Opportunities are becoming fewer, and before long, the season of service will be over. "As the dial at Abbotsford tells me, *Mox nox*: presently it will be night."[13]

Let us, therefore, be alert. Let us talk together as did Christian and Hopeful upon Enchanted Ground. (See *The Pilgrim's Progress.*] Let us keep one another awake to the prospects of glory, awake to the devices of Satan; awake to the need of a perishing world, awake to the responsibilities of our calling; until, at length, we reach the celestial city, where we shall work without wearying and rest without declining.

> Wake, brethren, wake!
> Jesus himself is nigh,
> Sleep is for sons of night,
> Ye are children of the light,
> Yours is the glory bright,
> Wake, brethren, wake![14]

---

12. Edward William Moore, *The Overcoming Life; or, Thoughts on the Life of Christ in the Soul of the Believer* (London, UK, 1885), 97–98.
13. Alexander Smellie, *On the Secret Place* (1907), 16.
14. "Watchman, What of the Night?" hymn by H. L. Hastings (1886).

THE WEAPON OF FAITH

"This is the victory that overcometh the world, even our faith" (1 John 5:4). Of course, there is no virtue in faith itself. The virtue is in the One faith links us to. Having the Son of God, the promises of God, and the Spirit of God, let us possess our possessions and use them against our common foe.

No room has been left in the divine program for devil-defeated lives. Our weapons are mighty, even to the pulling down of satanic strongholds, but we must appropriate these all-powerful weapons by faith, and use them against the enemy. Yes, and when we are strong in faith, then we know what it is to be a terror to the devil. Oh, to be feared by Satan! Oh, to live in God and by faith, so that he will cringe before our Spirit-inspired life and witness. Let us not forget that it is written: *"One* [should] *chase a thousand, and two put ten thousand to flight"* (Deuteronomy 32:30; see also Joshua 23:10). And so, no matter in what form we may have to meet the undying antagonism of Satan, may ours ever be the song of triumph. Thanks be unto God, who gives us the victory!

To Thee, and to Thy Christ, O God,
We sing, we ever sing;
For He the lonely wine-press trod,
Our cup of joy to bring.
His glorious arm the strife maintained,
He marched in might from far;
His robes were with the vintage stained,
Red with the wine of war.

To Thee and to Thy Christ, O God,
We sing, we ever sing;
For He invaded death's abode,
And robbed him of his sting.
The house of dust enthralls no more,
For He, the Strong to save,

Himself doth guard that silent door,
Great Keeper of the grave.

To Thee and to Thy Christ, O God,
We sing, we ever sing;
For He hath crushed beneath His rod
The world's proud rebel king;
He plunged in His imperial strength
To gulfs of darkness down;
He brought His trophy up at length,
The foiled usurper's crown.

To Thee and to Thy Christ, O God,
We sing, we ever sing;
For He redeemed us with His blood
From every evil thing.
Thy saving strength His arm upbore,
The arm that set us free:
Glory, O God, for evermore
Be to Thy Christ and Thee.[15]

15. "To Thee and to Thy Christ, O God," hymn by Anne R. Cousin (1876).

ABOUT THE AUTHOR

Dr. **Herbert Lockyer** (1886–1984) considered becoming an actor when he was first deciding on a career. Tall and well-spoken, he seemed a natural for the theater. But the Lord had something better in mind. Instead of the stage, God called Herbert to the pulpit, where, as a pastor, a Bible teacher, and the author of more than fifty books, he touched the hearts and lives of millions of people.

Dr. Lockyer held pastorates in Scotland and England for twenty-five years. As pastor of Leeds Road Baptist Church in Bradford, England, he became a leader in the Keswick Higher Life Movement, which emphasized the significance of living in the fullness of the Holy Spirit. This led to an invitation to speak at the Moody Bible Institute's fiftieth anniversary in 1936. His warm reception at that event led to his ministry in the United States. He received honorary degrees from both the Northwestern Evangelical Seminary and the International Academy in London.

In 1955, he returned to England, where he lived for many years. He then returned to the United States, where he spent the final years of his life in Colorado Springs, Colorado, with his son, the Rev. Herbert Lockyer Jr., a Presbyterian minister who eventually became his editor. He is best known for his two books: *All the Men of the Bible* and *All the Women of the Bible*. Other books with Whitaker House include *7 Pillars of God's Wisdom*, *Revelation: Drama of the Ages*, and *Seasons of the Lord: 365-Day Devotional*.